Do You Need a Miracle?

Dr. Sheila Hamlin

Written Words Publishing LLC
14189 E Dickinson Drive, Unit F
Aurora, CO 80014
www.writtenwordspublishing.com

Do You Need a Miracle? © 2022 by Dr. Sheila Hamlin.

All rights reserved. No part of this publication may be reproduced, stored in a retrieval system, or transmitted in any form by any means, electronic, mechanical, photocopying, recording, or otherwise, without the prior permission of the author.

Published by Written Words Publishing LLC August 9, 2022

ISBN: 978-1-7356856-7-0 (paperback)
ISBN: 978-1-7356856-8-7 (eBook)

Library of Congress Control Number: 2022913842

Cover designed by Written Words Publishing LLC

Manufactured and printed in the United States of America

All Scripture quotations, unless otherwise indicated, are taken from the King James Version of the Bible, public domain. Scripture quotations noted as NLT are taken from the Holy Bible, New Living Translation, Copyright © 1996, 2004, 2007. Used by permission of Tyndale House Publishers, Inc., Carol Stream, Illinois 60188. All rights reserved. Scripture quotations noted as NIV are taken from the Holy Bible, New International Version® NIV®. Copyright © 1973, 1978, 1984, 2011 by the International Bible Society. Used by permission of Zondervan Publishing House. All rights reserved worldwide. Scripture quotations noted as AMPC are taken from the Amplified® Bible, Classic Edition, Copyright © 2015 by The Lockman Foundation. Used by permission of The Lockman Foundation. All rights reserved worldwide. Scripture quotations noted as CSB have been taken from the Christian Standard Bible®, Copyright © 2017 by Holman Bible Publishers. Used by permission. Christian Standard Bible® and CSB® are federally registered trademarks of Holman Bible Publishers. Scripture quotations noted as MSG are taken from The Message. Copyright © 1993, 1994, 1995, 1996, 2000, 2001, 2002. Used by permission of NavPress Publishing Group. Scripture quotations noted as ESV are taken from The Holy Bible, English Standard Version®, Copyright © 2016 by Crossway Bibles, a division of Good News Publishers. Used by permission. All rights reserved. Scripture quotations noted as NKJV are taken from the New King James Version. Copyright © 1979, 1980, 1982 by Thomas Nelson, Inc. Used by permission. All rights reserved.

*Dedicated to my Lord Jesus,
my husband, and my daughters.*

Table of Contents

Chapter 1: A Loving Dad 1

Chapter 2: It's Easy for the Lord 5

Chapter 3: Who's Hungry 9

Chapter 4: No Abracadabra or Hocus Pocus 13

Chapter 5: No Smell of Smoke 17

Chapter 6: No Way Out 19

Chapter 7: A Resurrection or Two 23

Chapter 8: Don't Get in the Ditch 27

Chapter 9: My Testimony 31

Chapter 10: What You Need to Do! 35

The Conclusion 40

CHAPTER 1

A LOVING DAD

*"Behold, I am the LORD, the God of all flesh:
is there any thing too hard for me?"*
(Jeremiah 32:27)

So, is your back against the wall? Are you in desperate need of a miracle? Did you pick up this book as a last-ditch grasp of hope? Have you tried all your relatives and friends and finally—with nowhere else to turn—you have turned to God? Well, welcome! The Father greets you with open arms. You have come to the right place!

What?... Are you still standing at the threshold, afraid to come close? I understand. Truly, I do. You are looking at yourself, your flaws, mistakes, your laziness, or even sin. That focus can keep you from coming closer to get help from a Holy God. That's absolutely true, but just for a moment think of God as a loving Father, a parent.

Do you have children? Or are you the child of a loving parent? Stop and remember the last time your child was in trouble. NOTHING ELSE IN THE WORLD MATTERS WHEN YOUR CHILD IS IN TROUBLE! I heard a minister tell the story of her son being bullied by a neighboring kid. This son also had a chart on his bedroom door of the chores he needed to complete each week. However, when this boy was outside playing and the bully came around, he would holler for his dad. Guess what? Dad did not stop to check the chore-chart before hurrying outside to help his son. He did not say, "Well, Johnny, you did not make your bed yesterday morning, so I am going to let the bully pound on your head a while before I come to your rescue." No, no, a thousand times NO! Can't you see this dad bursting through the doorway accompanied with a loud shout saying, "Take your hands off my child!"

All Johnny had to do was cry out and he had the attention, power, and might of a loving father coming to his aid. You have a loving Father who is a very present help in time of trouble (Psalm 46:1).

So, you have not done everything right—nobody has. That's why Jesus came. In later chapters, we will examine our lives and make any needed adjustments but for now I want you to turn your eyes to a God that will rescue you in spite of yourself.

Psalm 107 paints a wonderful picture of God's heart toward his children. Over and over, it states the children of Israel cried unto the LORD and He delivered them.

> *"Then they cried unto the LORD in their trouble, and he delivered them out of their distresses"* (Psalm 107:6).

> *"Then they cried unto the LORD in their trouble, and he saved them out of their distresses"* (Psalm 107:13).

> *"Then they cry unto the LORD in their trouble, and he saveth them out of their distresses"* (Psalm 107:19).

> *"Then they cry unto the LORD in their trouble, and he bringeth them out of their distresses"* (Psalm 107:28).

There are other lessons in chapter 107 that we can expound upon, but I think the main message is clear. Again and again, there was trouble, and again and again there was deliverance from a loving God. The chapter closes with a great summary. The New Living Translation states, *"Those who are wise will take all this to heart; they will see in our history the faithful love of the LORD"* (Psalm 107:43 NLT).

God has a history of faithful love, a history of miracles. Is there a miracle for you? What's your answer? You do have a part to play in this. Right now, that part is hope. Hope is our starting point. It is not our end point. But, for the next few chapters, I want to get your hope up as high as a Georgia pine. Then will come faith. Next will come victory! Let's get started.

Chapter 2

It's Easy for the Lord

"Is any thing too hard for the Lord?..."
(Genesis 18:14)

There are so many miracles of God—where does one begin? Shall we talk about the three Hebrew boys in the fiery furnace, or Daniel in the lions' den? Those are great accounts of the power and *might* of our Loving God.

Hold it. Pause for a second. Before I share with you one of my favorites, I want you to notice the word I used—accounts. I did not say stories. These are Bible stories but too often when we say *stories* our brain thinks of fairy tales and fiction stories we have read or watched on television. No, these stories are true, actual accounts of real, live events of ~~Bible~~ history.

Reprogram your mind to read it like a news report. (Although many people do not trust the media these days—but you get my point!) I could give you some facts and figures to soothe the logical mind on why we can trust the Bible. Perhaps I will put it in a later book, but for now I want to tell you one of my favorite miracles. It is found in Second Kings chapter three.

Three kings and their armies were trekking through the wilderness to go into battle. After days of travel, they ran out of water. Just imagine, no water for all those soldiers, their horses or even the cattle that traveled with them.

There was a typical worrier among the group. You know the type—he falls apart and thinks the worst at the first sign of trouble. He said, "Oh no, God has led us out here to die!" (That's the Hamlin Paraphrased Version or HPV). Fortunately, the King of Judah kept his wits about him and said, *"Is there not here a prophet of the LORD, that we may enquire of the LORD by him?"* (2 Kings 3:11). The man of God came, received a Word from the LORD, and gave them a plan of action.

> *And he said, Thus saith the LORD, Make this valley full of ditches. For thus saith the LORD, Ye shall not see wind, neither shall ye see rain; yet that valley shall be filled with water, that ye may drink, both ye, and your cattle, and your beasts. And this is but a light thing in the sight of the LORD: he will deliver the Moabites also into your hand* (2 Kings 3:16-18).

"This is but a light thing." I love that! The NIV states, *"This is an easy thing in the eyes of the LORD."* Folks, this was not easy for them. This was potential life or death. Thousands upon thousands of troops without water. This did not just suddenly come upon them. I am sure that as they were traveling someone was watching the rations. Captains had been sending out scouts to the north, south, east, and west in search of water resources. They were probably digging for wells, searching for streams, and hunting for brooks. All to no avail.

Finally, they called on the LORD. They inquired of the prophet of the LORD. That's what you have done in picking up this book. Notice what the prophet did next. He called for a musician. I believe this represents a time of worship.

Perhaps you need to set aside some time to get alone with God. Play some songs of praise and adoration and block out the noise of the world. Focus on the majesty of God and not the mountain of your problems.

Focus on how good He is.

Focus on how loving He is.

Focus on how faithful He is and how faithful He has been.

God answered these kings in their time of need. His answer was supernatural. However, it was not loud or flashy. God told them, *"Ye shall not see wind, neither shall ye see rain; yet that valley shall be filled with water…"* (2 Kings 3:17). Water just appeared in the ditches without rain or wind. It was an awesome display of God's power without a dynamic show. Some people, in looking for the spectacular, may miss the supernatural.

There is another part to this miracle that we should not overlook. God gave them victory in the battle with the Moabites. They were seeking water; God gave them water *and* defeated their enemy. He gave them a two-for-one. The Moabite army saw the water as blood and thought the three armies had quarreled and destroyed themselves. They strolled into camp to plunder the spoils only to be attacked and defeated. Enemies beware; there's no victory for you when the children of God call out to their Heavenly Father in the time of battle.

What lessons can we learn from this passage? What did they do?

1. They called on the Lord.
2. The prophet called for a minstrel (musician).

3. The LORD gave them instructions. There was something they had to do.
4. God met their need.
5. God gave them more than they asked by defeating their enemies.

Keep your eyes open for any similar patterns in other miracles.

CHAPTER 3

WHO'S HUNGRY

"When you open your hand, you satisfy the hunger and thirst of every living thing."
(Psalm 145:16 NLT)

As we read these miracles of God, I want you to meditate on His power and provision. Place yourself in the midst of the miracle. In the events of the previous chapter, I see the armies rising in the morning, stepping out of their tents, and being amazed at the ditches filled with water. Forgetting all about order, rank and file, they run over, putting their faces in the water to quench their thirst. Ahh, the sweet taste of victory.

In my mind, there is a time factor for God to work on their behalf. He did it while they slept. However, with the miracle of the fish and loaves, I think to myself, *LORD, how did you do that?* There is no time factor for God to multiply the food. Read it here with me from the Gospel of St. Luke.

And when the day began to wear away, then came the twelve, and said unto him, Send the multitude away, that they may go into the towns and country round about, and lodge, and get victuals: for we are here in a desert place. But he said unto them, Give ye them to eat. And they said, We have no more but five loaves and two fishes; except we should go and buy meat for all this people. For they were about five thousand men. And he said to his disciples, Make them sit down by fifties in a company. And they did so, and made them all sit down. Then he took the five loaves and the two fishes, and looking up to heaven, he blessed them, and brake, and gave to the disciples to set before the multitude. And they did eat, and were all filled: and there was taken up of fragments that remained to them twelve baskets (Luke 9:12-17).

Jesus fed over five thousand with a few fish and loaves of bread. Remember what I said about the time factor. There was none. The food went from Jesus' hands to the disciple—to the people. Wow, what a God we serve! He is a God of miracles.

Are you in a tight spot? Is there a time crunch? Look to Jesus. Look to your Heavenly Father. He can make a way that our finite minds cannot fathom.

One of the things I like about this miracle is that it is not a life-or-death situation. Yes, it was good and needed but they could have walked home. However, that was not God's heart. Jesus is willing to do miracles even just to make it convenient. That might put a wrinkle in some people's brain, but it is right there in black and white (or maybe in red in your Bible).

Jesus is meeting the needs of the multitude. Can you see yourself in the crowd? Can you see any scoundrels in the crowd? Come on, if it is a crowd of over five thousand, there are bound to be some of *ill repute* among them all. Some who just came out of curiosity; some came to be critical. They all were fed, saint and sinner alike!

Where do you fit in the crowd? Are you a child of the Most High God or are you a wayward stranger looking for a hand-out? Notice, Jesus did not turn anyone away. In fact, He bids all to come to Him who are burdened down with problems (Matthew 11:28). In Him, we can find real rest.

In summary of this event, they had a problem and they went to Jesus. He gave them a plan of action—sit down in companies of fifty. Next, we see prayer, provision, and overflow. Not only did He multiply the fish and loaves for more than five thousand, but there were also fragments left over, enough to fill several baskets. This happened again in the ministry of Jesus. In the next case, four thousand were fed. In both accounts, there was an abundant supply with baskets of food remaining. That is the God I serve. He can do exceedingly abundantly above all we can ask or think (Ephesians 3:20).

CHAPTER 4

NO ABRACADABRA OR HOCUS POCUS

"...In the world you have tribulation and trials and distress and frustration; but be of good cheer [take courage; be confident, certain, undaunted]! For I have overcome the world. [I have deprived it of power to harm you and have conquered it for you.]"
(John 16:33 AMPC)

Since we talked about time in the last chapter, let's talk about the fact that God's supernatural work is not like rubbing a magic lantern. He is not your genie in a bottle, and we do not use the name of Jesus like a magic wand. Television has marred and scarred us for dealing with the supernatural. Some think answers to prayer should appear instantly like TV magic. If we do not see our provision or healing immediately, God doesn't exist or maybe He said no. Resist those erroneous conclusions. Sometimes, victory is a process. We can see this in the life of Jesus and the miracles He performed.

In the Gospel of Mark chapter eight, we read the account of Jesus healing a blind man.

And he cometh to Bethsaida; and they bring a blind man unto him, and besought him to touch him. And he took the blind man by the hand, and led him out of the town; and when he had spit on his eyes, and put his hands upon him, he asked him if he saw ought.

And he looked up, and said, I see men as trees, walking. After that he put his hands again upon his eyes, and made him look up: and he was restored, and saw every man clearly (Mark 8:22-25).

Look at that. A notable miracle has been done by the hands of Jesus, and yet it was not instantaneous. Look now at the account of the ten lepers.

And as he entered into a certain village, there met him ten men that were lepers, which stood afar off: And they lifted up their voices, and said, Jesus, Master, have mercy on us. And when he saw them, he said unto them, Go shew yourselves unto the priests. And it came to pass, that, as they went, they were cleansed (Luke 17:12-14).

Notice in this account it said they were cleansed as they went. We do not know how far they had traveled—a few steps or a few miles. Most important to note is they took Jesus at His word and began acting in obedience to go to the priest. Under Jewish law, lepers could present themselves to the priest after being healed in order to enter back into society (Leviticus 14:2). These ten lepers could have yelled back to Jesus, "Hey, heal us first and then we can go!" Thank goodness they followed instructions and received the miraculous.

Will you receive your miracle from the Lord? Have you been given instructions that you need to follow? Or are you sitting around waiting on Jesus? He might be waiting on you. Check your heart; ask the Holy Spirit if there is something you need to do. If you have done all you can do and you have God's promise to stand on, then it might be time to just stand. Be unmovable; wait patiently to see God's faithfulness.

It is important not to get in the ravine on either side of the miraculous. Read now some of the instant miracles of Jesus.

> *And, behold, there came a leper and worshipped him, saying, Lord, if thou wilt, thou canst make me clean. And Jesus put forth his hand, and touched him, saying, I will; be thou clean. And immediately his leprosy was cleansed* (Matthew 8:2,3).

I like that word *immediately*. How about you? Let's observe it again as Jesus heals.

> *And forthwith, when they were come out of the synagogue, they entered into the house of Simon and Andrew, with James and John. But Simon's wife's mother lay sick of a fever, and anon they tell him of her. And he came and took her by the hand, and lifted her up; and immediately the fever left her, and she ministered unto them* (Mark 1:29-31).

There is the word we love to see—immediately. Yes, we serve a God who does immediate wonders.

> *And, behold, two blind men sitting by the way side, when they heard that Jesus passed by, cried out, saying, Have mercy on us, O Lord, thou Son of David. And the multitude rebuked them, because they should hold their peace: but they cried the more, saying, Have mercy on us, O Lord, thou Son of David. And Jesus stood still, and called them, and said, What will ye that I shall do unto you? They say*

unto him, Lord, that our eyes may be opened. So Jesus had compassion on them, and touched their eyes: and immediately their eyes received sight, and they followed him (Matthew 20:30-34).

Some of the works of Jesus have been instantaneous and some have been a process. Knowing this teaches us that we must listen for the voice of the Holy Spirit and allow Him to work in our lives and do the supernatural as only God can. We do not have to figure out how; our part is to trust. We must trust the integrity of God's Word and His character.

There is an Old Testament account of Israel fighting against another nation. God was giving Israel the victory. The enemy army made the mistake of thinking they had figured God out. They said, "Oh, their God must be the God of the hills; let's get them in the valley and we can beat them" (That's the Hamlin Paraphrased Version again). Big mistake. They garrisoned up their forces to come against God's people. On the field of battle, it looked like certain defeat for Israel. The Bible says they looked like *"two little flocks of goats, while the Arameans filled the landscape"* (1 Kings 20:27 CSB). The Message Bible says, *"The plain was seething with Arameans"* (1 King 20:27). You do know how this turned out, right? God showed Himself strong and the Israelites gained a great success. They slew 100,000 footmen in one day! Truly, He is God of the hills and God of the valley. No matter where you are today, call on this Great God and let Him show Himself strong on your behalf.

Chapter 5

No Smell of Smoke

"He shall call upon me, and I will answer him: I will be with him in trouble; I will deliver him, and honour him."
(Psalm 91:15)

One cannot write a book of Bible miracles and not talk about the three Hebrew children in the fiery furnace. If you were raised like I was, you may have heard the account in Sunday School or in a good-ole country revival meeting. No matter when you heard it or how often you've read it, this account always inspires and encourages.

Turn to chapter three in the book of Daniel. King Nebuchadnezzar of Babylon set up a golden statue of himself for all to bow down and worship. All the leaders, governors and rulers were invited to the dedication ceremony. Three young men, Shadrach, Meshach and Abednego, chose not to bow down to worship the statue. This made King Nebuchadnezzar furious. One translation said, "his face purple with anger" (Daniel 3:19 MSG). Okay, that's pretty bad. As punishment, Nebuchadnezzar ordered them to be thrown in a fiery furnace that was so hot the flames consumed the guards that threw them in!

And these three men, Shadrach, Meshach, and Abednego, fell down bound into the midst of the burning fiery furnace. Then Nebuchadnezzar the king was astonished, and rose up in haste, and spake, and said unto his counsellors, Did not we cast three men bound into the midst of the fire? They answered and said unto the king, True, O king. He answered and said, Lo, I see four men loose, walking in the midst of the fire, and they have no hurt; and the form of the fourth is like the Son of God. Then Nebuchadnezzar came near to the mouth of the burning fiery furnace, and spake, and said, Shadrach, Meshach, and Abednego, ye servants of the most high God, come forth, and come hither. Then Shadrach, Meshach, and Abednego, came forth of the midst of the fire. And the princes, governors, and captains, and the king's counsellors, being gathered together, saw these men, upon whose bodies the fire had no power, nor was an hair of their head singed, neither were their coats changed, nor the smell of fire had passed on them (Daniel 3:23-27).

Ha, ha on you Mr. King. So much for your ego, your decree and your rage. These men stood up for God's ways and God delivered them and changed the heart of the entire nation. If you are not shouting after that passage, your wood is wet. Also, there is such great detail in this account. My favorite is *not an hair of their head was singed*. It also says, *nor the smell of fire*. That's the power of God.

God can deliver in such a way that there is no residue of the problem in your midst. Set your sights on this kind of victory. Not only did God get glorified but Shadrach, Meshach and Abednego got promoted in the province of Babylon. Only our God can deliver in such a manner, and He has not changed.

Chapter 6

No Way Out

"God can do anything, you know—far more than you could ever imagine or guess or request..."
(Ephesians 3:20 MSG)

Our God specializes in making a way where there seems to be no way. Surely Moses can attest to this as he faced the Red Sea in front of him and Pharoah's army charging from the rear. Once again, I implore you to put yourself among the tribes of Israel as they journey out of Egypt. They begin the trip with happy anticipation, breathing in the air of freedom. Remember, these men, mothers and children have been in bondage all their lives. Surely the camps were full of singing and rejoicing until...someone hears the rumbling of army chariots. Next, they see the dust cloud of raging horses. Pharoah's horses. Fear seizes the hearts at the sight of Pharoah's chariots. Panic rips through the crowd like a tidal wave. With the Red Sea in front of them and Pharoah's army behind them, seemingly there is no place to go. This has to be a prime example of being between a rock and a hard place.

We read it now knowing the outcome but, in their eyes, this had to be an impossible situation. Surely this is cause for panic and alarm. Is *your* situation this bad? Does there seem to be NO WAY OUT for you?

Look at the advice given to the children of Israel. *"But Moses told the people, 'Don't be afraid. Just stand still and watch the LORD rescue you today...'"* (Exodus 14:13 NLT). God came through for them. He parted the Red Sea and the children of Israel walked through on dry ground. Then, in true God-like fashion, He gave them more. He told them the enemy you see today will pursue you no more. After the Israelites crossed on dry ground, Pharoah's army followed them and drowned as the wall of water returned into the sea. The entire army was defeated. God had delivered His children from an impossible situation. Hallelujah!! Let's pause here for a praise break and be thankful that we serve a God of miracles.

The next passage I want to discuss may not be described as a miracle, but it definitely fits under the "no way out" description. It is found in John 8:2-11. The scribes and the pharisees are trying to corner Jesus to discredit Him in the eyes of the people. They bring to Him a woman caught in the act of adultery. (I know you are thinking like me, where is the man? Right? Focus, that discussion would lead us to speculation). This is a very good plot on the part of the religious leaders. If Jesus says to stone the woman as the law demands, it will turn the people against Him. If He says let her go, that will show disrespect for the Law of God, and the Pharisees can use that against Him as well. What is He going to do? How does He honor God's Law and show compassion for God's people? Quite a dilemma, but not too much for God. Read the conclusion.

They say unto him, Master, this woman was taken in adultery, in the very act. Now Moses in the law commanded us, that such should be stoned: but what sayest thou? This they said, tempting him, that they might have to accuse him. But Jesus stooped down, and with his finger wrote on the ground, as though he heard them not. So when they continued asking him, he lifted up himself, and said unto them, He that is without sin among you, let him first cast a stone at her. And again he stooped down, and wrote on the ground. And they which heard it, being convicted by their own conscience, went out one by one, beginning at the eldest, even unto the last: and Jesus was left alone, and the woman standing in the midst (John 8:4-9).

See the wisdom of God in manifestation. Glory! That was absolutely brilliant. No one would have thought of that. That was downloaded straight from heaven. It serves as a glorious example to us. God has solutions, discoveries, and escape routes that our brains have not considered, and our hearts have not imagined. So, when you are backed against the wall, don't compromise to save your own skin. Look to God. Let Him rescue you. The scripture says, with every temptation you are faced with, God will make *"a way to escape"* (1 Corinthians 10:13). Look for it. Expect it. Receive help from heaven.

I remember a time when I had parked on the side of the road to attend an event. As I returned to the vehicle, the car keys fell in a manhole. Oh, my goodness, how quickly the mind flies to rapid-firing panic! What am I going to do? How am I going to get home? This is an old car; I don't have another set of keys. This means no keys to get in the house! STOP! I had to look to the LORD. "Father, what's your way of escape for me?" A revelation from heaven came to me... "Look in the manhole." It was bone-dry, with a ledge for me to stand on. Now it sounds humorous, but at the time it was quite serious. I was broke, and any extra expense was a major catastrophe. Thank goodness for God. He can turn mountains to molehills.

It's your turn. Time to look to the Jesus, look to your Heavenly Father. Find the way of escape He has already prepared for you.

Chapter 7

A Resurrection or Two

*"I cry out to God Most High,
to God, who vindicates me."*
(Psalm 57:2 NIV)

Do you realize that, with all our advanced technology, scientists cannot put life back into a dead fly? Think about that. We can fly to the moon, take pictures with our phone and change the temperature in our house from a remote location. But we cannot raise the dead. Jesus can and He did.

The Bible tells us that there was a funeral procession that Jesus interrupted. The dead man was the only child of a widow woman. Jesus called life back to his body and returned him to his mother (Luke 7:12-15). Wow, look at the miracle-working power of my loving Lord. But wait, there was no prayer, there were no instructions. How do we apply this to our lives? Do we sit back with our arms folded, moping and hoping that God might zap us with His power? No, we cannot do that.

The Bible says, *"All scripture is given by inspiration of God, and is profitable for doctrine, for reproof, for correction, for instruction in righteousness:"* (2 Timothy 3:16). So, what is the instruction in this miracle? It is clear—we serve a God of power and a God of compassion. We remind ourselves that we serve a God of power and compassion. We remind our problem that we serve a God of power and compassion. He is the same yesterday and forever, according to Hebrews 13:8. If He raised the dead back then, He can do the same today. If He healed the sick back then, He can do the same today.

In the Second Book of Kings, we see the resurrection power of God on display yet again. This is an odd account. They threw a dead man on the bones of the prophet Elisha and the dead man revived (2 Kings 13:21). That is amazing. That is the power of the anointing at work.

That same anointing flowed through Jesus. He operated in the gifts of the Holy Spirit and demonstrated the will and the power of the Father. We are called to be His disciples, His followers, and His examples in the earth. How can we access this power? Jesus said, *"He that believeth on me, the works that I do shall he do also..."* (John 14:12).

Whoa, that's a tall order. Jesus raised the dead not once, not twice, but three times in His earthly ministry! How do we follow that example? Read closely what He said—*believe* on me. We've got to change our mindset to believe what Jesus said more than what our senses say. That's the purpose of this book to read, ponder and meditate on the Word and works of Jesus to build our faith.

It is not enough to build up our faith, we also must decrease our unbelief. That may sound like two sides of the same coin, but it is not exactly. Think of it as a sink with the faucet turned on. It would be easy to fill up the sink; but if the plug is out at the bottom, then the water would simply go down the drain. According to the Word, faith comes by hearing the Word of God (Romans 10:17);

likewise, you can say that doubt and unbelief come by hearing words contrary to God. Words from the television, radio, internet, neighbors, newspapers, unbelieving lawyers, doctors, and/or insurance salesmen fill us with unbelief. We are daily bombarded with these worldly words that pull against our faith like a sink with no plug that lets all the water run out. We must put the Word in and not allow the world to drain it all out. If you need a miracle, you will need to turn off the world and **tune in** the Word.

We may not need to raise the dead, but maybe bring resurrection to a dream. Perhaps we need to revive a dead marriage or resuscitate a lifeless career. Don't despair, believe. The Bible says that Abraham believed God in the midst of a dead situation. He was 99-years old, married to a barren old woman; yet he had a promise from God that he would be the father of many nations. He believed God's promise more than the deadness of his own body and Abraham and Sarah gave birth to that promised seed. He believed in *"...the God who gives life to the dead...."* (Romans 4:17 NIV). If Abraham can have a resurrection, then so can you and me. Let's believe God's Word more than any contrary circumstance.

Chapter 8

Don't Get in the Ditch

"...Stick with what you learned and believed,...There's nothing like the written Word of God for showing you the way to salvation...Through the Word we are put together and shaped up for the tasks God has for us."
(2 Timothy 3:14-17 MSG)

Too often, when people face a crisis, they jump in the ditch of fear. The bad report hits the ears. The heart starts beating fast, the imagination forms a worst-case scenario and unfortunately, too many people open their mouths and say words that are not God-inspired. STOP. Speak peace to your emotions, speak peace to your imagination. Say out loud, "MY GOD IS BIGGER THAN THIS SITUATION!" If you are in a crowded room, whisper it to yourself, but you do need to say something. Arrest the thoughts of your mind with the words of your mouth.

I heard a minister say, *first words count*. I like that. What is the first thing out of your mouth? Are you releasing power and faith? Or are you using words that curse and defame your God? The Bible says, *"...out of the abundance of the heart the mouth speaks"* (Matthews 12:34 NJKV). You can tell what's in your heart in abundance by those first words. Have you ever stubbed your toe walking through a dark room? Whatever is in you, is going to come out of you.

My daughter and I went to the movies with some friends. She sat with her friend several rows away from me, but when there was a sudden fright on the screen, she heard these words loudly in the theater, "*JESUS!*" and said to herself, "that's my momma!" I couldn't help it. I didn't think it up. It just came out. Take time to put the Word of God in your heart. It will be there when you need it.

Some say we were designed so that at a time of crisis our minds can shut down and allow our spirit-man to take over. The problem comes when our spirits have not been reborn or have not been nourished with God's Word and therefore when the mind shuts down there is nothing left to sustain us. That's called a nervous break-down. People, we need to feed on the Word daily. We are a spirit; we have a soul; and we live in a physical body (1 Thessalonians 5:23). We need to nurture the whole man in order to live healthy and victorious lives on the earth. What did God say about your situation? That's what **you** need to say. Say it loud and say it proud.

I grew up in the country and I have walked down a lot of country roads. Guess what? There is a ditch on both sides of the road. Likewise, there are two ditches we can encounter in a crisis. One is fear; the other is neglect. The latter is harder to identify because there is a fine line between neglect and turning your cares over to the Lord. This is where prayer and fellowship with the Father and with the Holy Spirit will help you know the difference. First Peter 5:7 tells us to cast our care upon the Lord, but let's look at that verse in context with the verses before and after it.

Humble yourselves therefore under the mighty hand of God, that he may exalt you in due time: Casting all your care upon him; for he careth for you. Be sober, be vigilant; because your adversary the devil, as a roaring lion, walketh about, seeking whom he may devour: Whom resist stedfast in the faith... (1 Peter 5:6-9).

Our first instruction in this passage is to humble ourselves before the LORD. Secondly, we are told to cast our care upon the LORD. And thirdly, we are told to resist the devil. Some folks only follow steps three and two—in that order. What about step one? Humble yourself under the mighty hand of God! How do we do this? We look at who HE IS! Run to the ROCK! Consider HIM and His Power, His Provision, His Protection!!! Get HIM on your mind first!! *Look-a-here problem, you are not bigger than my GOD!* HE SPLIT THE RED SEA! HE RAISED THE DEAD! HE BROUGHT WATER OUT OF A ROCK! HE DIED FOR ME AND WAS RAISED FROM THE DEAD WITH ALL POWER IN HIS HAND!! This is step one.

The act of being humble carries the connotation of lowering oneself. In this case, we are lowering or submitting ourselves to the Most High God, acknowledging that He has all power and all wisdom for the situation we may find ourselves facing. Depending on the timing, we may humble ourselves through fasting, worship or quiet fellowship—just listening for His instructions.

After receiving and following instructions, then comes the "casting the care." Be purposeful about this. I think some people just rattle off some words in the air and call it prayer. That's what I call neglect. I want you to get out your Bible. Open to this passage and go before the LORD in quiet reverence. Listen for the Holy Spirit. Let Him lead your prayer before the Father. This cannot be scripted. It needs to be Word-based and Spirit-led.

Next, this passage admonishes us to be sober and vigilant. In other words, this is work, keeping your mind (and your mouth) off the problem. The enemy of your thoughts will ask you a thousand times, *whadaya going to do*? This calls for vigilance to NOT pick up that care. Write a scripture on a card and keep it in your pocket. Get a Word-based song and keep singing in your mind. This is how we resist the devil. This is how we win.

We live in an earth-cursed system. Bad things happen to good people. However, the children of God can live free from the curse (Galatians 3:13). We must follow natural laws *and* we must follow spiritual laws. We cannot jump off buildings and try to defy the law of gravity. We cannot make good confessions yet fail to obey the leading of the Holy Spirit. We also cannot give our cares to God in prayer and then pick them back up and tell everyone how worried we are. No, no, a thousand times no.

Plan to win. Prepare a God-inspired response to those who may question you about the problem (1 Peter 3:15). Don't come across religious to your worldly co-workers. But prepare an answer that will keep you in faith and shut them up quickly. Then walk around with a smile until it is time to testify that God indeed has rescued you from discomfort, disease or disaster.

Chapter 9

My Testimony

*"For all the promises of God in Him
are Yes, and in Him Amen..."*
(2 Corinthians 1:20 NKJV)

I sat in the doctor's office and heard these words, "You have Trisomy 18 known as Edward Syndrome. You've heard of Down Syndrome, right? Well, people do not know of Edward Syndrome because babies with Edward Syndrome don't survive. They *may* make it to the third trimester; but few live beyond the first year..." After that, her words went blurry and so did my eyes. Emotions were raging, tears were flowing but my heart was established in the power of my God. The doctor wanted to do some other invasive procedure. I told her, "No, we believe in God." Her reply, "OK, just show me a healthy baby, show me a healthy baby." From that point, the fight was on. Morning and night, thoughts of despair and death waged against the hopes and joys. God's Word promised me life. I had to stand.

I had married late in life and became pregnant. The doctor termed me as a "mature" pregnancy. I won't say how old I was, but my aunt said, *"I know she ain't trying to have no baby as old as she is!"* referring to me. (Make sure you use a high-pitched shrill as you read that last comment). I figured if Sarah could have a baby at 89 with a miracle from God, then the same God could help me. It just was not going to be easy.

I went to see my general practitioner who was a believer. He pulled out a medical source and read all the other things that could be wrong with my baby—things like organs being displaced throughout the body or nub fingers. Then he asked me what I was going to do. I looked at him like he was crazy. "I'm going to believe God!" I replied. I was saying in my head, "What do you think? Why even ask me that?" I guess he was locating me. Sometimes you must locate yourself. Are you believing to come through an operation or believing not to *need* the operation? Only you can answer those kinds of questions.

The choice was clear for me. I wasn't playing church. This God I serve is real and He really loves me. There are precious promises in His Word that Jesus Christ has borne all my sickness and carried all my diseases, that included Trisomy 18. There are promises in His Word that I can have life and have it more abundantly, that includes life for the unborn child I was carrying. The doctor's report did not agree with God's Covenant promises.

The fifty-third chapter of Isaiah opens with a question, *"Who has believed our report?"* (Isaiah 53:1 NKJV). I had to answer that question. I believe the report of the LORD. I resist the report of the doctor. I did not go into a long litany with the medical doctors. I did not rebuke the doctors. In fact, I never said another word about my faith in all my follow-up visits. I just kept believing. When they said I wasn't gaining weight in my third trimester, I just kept believing. When they said I had gestational diabetes, I just kept believing. So, when I tell you to stand on God's Word,

I am telling you something that I have been through. Standing through tears, standing through fears—I just kept believing.

I had a song that I would sing to my unborn child every day, a song of life, a song of hope! "I Speak Life" by Donald Lawrence. I cannot hear that song now without tearing up. It seems like it was written just for me in the time of trouble. God also sent me a Word of encouragement through Christian television. I was watching a broadcast where the host and guest have dialogue. I seldom watch this type of Christian TV; normally I watch a sermon from a preacher. However, this television show was on, and the man of God said a word for me. He said you will have a baby girl. (I didn't know it was a girl at that time.) She will live and not die and declare the works of the LORD. Hallelujah! I did have a daughter and God did make her every bit healthy and whole! THANK YOU, LORD JESUS.

I have said for years, things you get with your faith, have a greater anointing on them. Think about it. Consider the biblical accounts where the mothers had to pray and ask for God's help to have a child; the child was special. Hannah prayed for Samuel—he was anointed. Moses' mom had to pray over him as she sent him afloat in the river. He was mightily used by God. John the Baptist was born out of a miracle (probably from Elizabeth's faith). He was a great prophet of God. Likewise, I had to pray for my daughter's life and God has blessed her. She is an outstanding student—an Honor roll student with perfect scores on State Standardized test, and among the highest scores in the county on the PSAT (Preliminary Scholastic Aptitude Test). One of her teachers declared that she is the smartest child she has ever taught. As a high school sophomore, she is already receiving interest letters from Harvard and Yale. It is only by God's grace. We are going to keep on believing to see what great works God will do in her life.

Chapter 10

What You Need to Do!

*"...Believe in the L*ORD* your God, and you will be established; believe his prophets, and you will succeed."*
(2 Chronicles 20:20 ESV)

Have you ever watched those infomercials that promise the remedy to some ailment in only two minutes if you just click the button below? I have watched and I have clicked. Twenty minutes later, I'm still waiting for the answer. So frustrating. I am not going to do that. I started this book with a question and now I am answering it. The answer is to SEEK GOD. That's it. Seek God because He alone knows all your problems and solutions, even the intricate, hidden, spiritual details that **you** do not know. I cannot give you a formula, a magic prayer, or a quick fix. I do not know if you need healing or deliverance, money, or restoration. Only He knows.

Seeking equals time. If you had rattlesnakes in your living quarters, you would stop everything and take the time needed to get rid of them. Yet we seldom want to take time to seek God for His divine wisdom. We live in such a *microwave-fastfood*-era that it is often difficult to quiet oneself to hear from heaven. It can be done through time in the Word, time in worship, time in prayer, and time in praise.

In years past, I would have told you to just get God's Word concerning your situation and hold to it firmer than the word of a lawyer, doctor or trusted friend. That's still true but often there is something we need to do; these instructions come from the Holy Spirit. Listening for His voice is a vital step toward victory. However, it can be hard to hear His voice with the television screaming or the YouTube videos playing. We must shut the world out and let the voice of God come in and give us counsel and direction.

There is an account in Second Chronicles that really shows all the points we have been discussing. My pastor from many years back preached a message from this passage. His title was *What to Do When You Don't Know What to Do*. I don't remember his points, but the Holy Spirit can still teach us from King Jehoshaphat's dilemma.

Many armies had gathered together to come against Judah. *"And Jehoshaphat feared, and set himself to seek the Lord, and proclaimed a fast throughout all Judah"* (2 Chronicles 20:3). The whole nation stopped what they were doing and came together. *"And Judah gathered themselves together, to ask help of the LORD: even out of all the cities of Judah they came to seek the LORD"* (2 Chronicles 20:4). Can you imagine if our whole nation shut down to seek help from the LORD? We shut down for a pandemic, why not for a prayer service? Jehoshaphat did and it brought him great results.

Notice how Jehoshaphat prayed. He did not begin his prayer with the problem. He began by acknowledging the greatness of God. Next, he reminded God of His covenant with Abraham. Let's read.

...O LORD God of our fathers, art not thou God in heaven? and rulest not thou over all the kingdoms of the heathen? and in thine hand is there not power and might, so that none is able to withstand thee? Art not thou our God, who didst drive out the inhabitants of this land before thy people Israel, and gavest it to the seed of Abraham thy friend for ever? (2 Chronicles 20:6,7).

The reference to Abraham thy friend is the same as reminding God of His Word, which is His covenant. Their covenant was through Abraham; our better covenant is through Christ Jesus. This is how we should pray. The entire account points out every principle I mentioned earlier in the book. I did not have this in my outline. I just thought of it as I wrote the chapter title and remembered the old sermon. (Sounds like a Holy Ghost set up just for you.) This is outstanding. Look at how they humbled themselves in verse 12, *"...we have no might against this great company that cometh against us; neither know we what to do: but our eyes are upon thee."* This is coming out of the mouth of the king. He is not putting on a brave facade in front of the people. He laid it all out and God came to the rescue. The Spirit of the LORD answered, *"...Hearken ye, all Judah, and ye inhabitants of Jerusalem, and thou king Jehoshaphat, Thus saith the LORD unto you, Be not afraid nor dismayed by reason of this great multitude; for the battle is not yours, but God's"* (verse 15). That's a word of solace—the battle is not yours but God's.

Some of you have heard that saying in a song and didn't know where it originated. The Spirit of the LORD went on to give them instructions—telling them specifically where to go and added:

> *Ye shall not need to fight in this battle: set yourselves, stand ye still, and see the salvation of the LORD with you, O Judah and Jerusalem: fear not, nor be dismayed; to morrow go out against them: for the LORD will be with you* (2 Chronicles 20:17).

I like those instructions—sweatless victory! I am calling for some of that right now in my life. How about you? What Jehoshaphat did next was also crucial. He began to worship. He bowed his face to the ground and the people followed his example. Here is the king prostrating himself before the true King of Kings and LORD of Lords. They bowed in worship and then stood up to praise (verse 18-19). This is how faith acts. God has told us what He is going to do. We believe it. We receive it, so let us rejoice!

They were so confident that God would do what He said, they put the praisers in front of the army! Wow, imagine that! They went out to battle singing, *"Praise the LORD for His mercy endureth forever"* (verse 21). While they were praising, the LORD caused the enemies to defeat themselves. By the time the children of Judah arrived at the battleground, there were only dead bodies and plenty of spoils. In true God-like fashion, He not only gave them victory over the enemy, but they got so much plunder (precious jewels) it took them three days to gather all the goods. Remember, it was **three** armies that had banded together. That should teach us not to look at the size of the problem, just consider the size of the bounty!

That's it, folks. Get your Bible out and read this entire account. Read it several times in several different versions. Then apply the principles. I did not want to give you a set formula, but I cannot argue with the Holy Ghost and the principles apparent in the Word. Seek Him. Obey Him. Then shout your way to victory and don't forget to gather up the spoils.

THE CONCLUSION: THE CAVEAT

Sorry guys, I forgot to tell you something—a very important detail. All these Scriptures and Covenant promises that I have written throughout this book are for everyone who has become a member of God's family. Yes, this loving Father takes care of His own children that come to Him in faith. However, we are not *all* born as children of God. We must be *born again* to be His children. This loving God that I have been talking about loved us so much that He sent His only Son to die for us. This whole human race has a sin nature, and it separates us from God. He is Holy and we are not. Nevertheless, this Holy God fixed the problem of sin and separation by sending Jesus to take our place. Will you say this simple prayer and join the family of God?

Prayer of Salvation and Dedication

Dear God in Heaven, I come to You to join Your family. I believe the record of Your son, Jesus Christ. He came to the earth and died for me. I believe all my wrongs were placed on Him. He went to hell for me, and You raised Him from the dead. Thank You, Lord Jesus. Come into my heart. I make You the Lord of my life and I dedicate myself to serve You now and for eternity. In Jesus' Name, Amen.

About the Author

Dr. Sheila Hamlin is a student of God's Word. Raised in a Baptist Church in rural Virginia, she continues to study and teach beyond denominational walls. She has an undergraduate degree from Virginia Union University; CAGS (Certificate of Advanced Graduate Studies) from Regent University; and a Ph.D. in Christian Education from Northwestern Theological Seminary. She was ordained in the ministry at FAIM (Faith Alive International Ministry) where she served for twenty years.

CPSIA information can be obtained
at www.ICGtesting.com
Printed in the USA
BVHW030223190922
647386BV00013B/431